BUNKER HILL

THE STORY TOLD IN LETTERS FROM THE BATTLEFIELD

View of the Attack on Bunker's Hill, with the Burning of Charles Town, June 17th 1775.

A Boston Battery | B Charles Town | C British Troops attacking | D Provincial Lines

BUNKER HILL:

THE STORY TOLD IN LETTERS FROM THE BATTLE FIELD

BY BRITISH OFFICERS ENGAGED.

WITH AN INTRODUCTION AND SKETCH OF THE BATTLE,

BY

SAMUEL ADAMS DRAKE,

AUTHOR OF "OLD LANDMARKS OF BOSTON," "HISTORIC FIELDS AND MANSIONS
OF MIDDLESEX," "NOOKS AND CORNERS OF THE
NEW ENGLAND COAST," ETC.

———oo¦●¦o-o———

BOSTON:

NICHOLS AND HALL.

1875.

Cambridge:
Press of John Wilson and Son.

BUNKER HILL

BY

SAMUEL ADAMS DRAKE

As Published in 1875

Digital Scanning and Publishing is a leader in the electronic republication of historical books and documents. We publish many of our titles as eBooks , paperback and hardcover editions. DSI is committed to bringing many traditional and well-known books back to life, retaining the look and feel of the original work.

Trade Paperback ISBN: 1-58218-329-5
Hardcover ISBN: 1-58218-330-9

©2008 DSI Digital Reproduction
First DSI Printing: November 2008

Published by Digital Scanning Inc. Scituate, MA 02066
781-545-2100 http://www.Digitalscanning.com *and*
http://www.PDFLibrary.com

TO

THE BRAVE MEN

WHOSE VALOR, PATRIOTISM, AND DEVOTION

HAVE RENDERED THE

SACRIFICES OF THEIR FATHERS

NOT UNAVAILING.

CONTENTS.

INTRODUCTION.

"Borne over the Atlantic, to the closing ear of Louis, king by the grace of God, what sounds are these; muffled, ominous, new in our centuries? Boston Harbor is black with unexpected Tea; behold a Pennsylvanian Congress gather; and ere long, on Bunker Hill, DEMOCRACY announcing, in rifle-volleys death-winged, under her Star Banner, to the tune of Yankee-doodle-doo, that she is born, and, whirlwind-like, will envelop the whole world!"—CARLYLE.

THE story of the battle of Bunker Hill has been told until it has become more familiar to American readers than Marathon or Waterloo. No subsequent field of the War for Independence possesses an equal interest with this first and fiercest grapple for the mastery. The unparalleled audacity of the seizure of the heights of Charlestown, in the presence of a numerous and powerful army and fleet; the unflinching firmness with which the Americans awaited the attack; the terrible loss inflicted on the enemy, unexampled on any later battle-field of the Revolution; and, finally, the curious spectacle of undisciplined yeomanry, without a leader known and respected as such, contesting with a veteran army and experienced officers, are marked features that at once suggest themselves to the student of the battle, and have rendered it for all time a memorable deed of arms.

The achievement of a century since that day offers a fitting occasion for the publication of materials that have

hitherto slumbered in the archives of British regiments
engaged on the field of Bunker Hill,—so long remem-
bered for the carnage in their ranks,—the mournful
theme of many a camp-fire during the war. These
fragments that have hitherto escaped the research of
historians of the battle, constitute the only apology the
author has to offer for the appearance of his pages as a
memorial of the Centennial Anniversary. The sketch
of the battle itself will have fulfilled its purpose in re-
freshing the recollections of the reader. Author and
reader are now too far removed from the event to feel
either lingering vindictiveness toward the enemy of a
century ago, or to be influenced by local prejudices
in awarding full honor where it is due.

At the time of the battle Boston and Charlestown
occupied two jutting peninsulas, widely separated at
their junction with the mainland, but approaching at
their extremities within less than half a mile of each
other. The river Charles flows between them, while
the Mystic separates Charlestown from the northern
shores of Boston harbor. Both streams are navigable
for large vessels a few miles up. The surface of both
peninsulas is broken into hills of no great elevation,—
those of Charlestown terminating the range approaching from the direction of Cambridge, which became the
American line of investment after the battle. The
topographical features of Boston and Charlestown have
undergone important changes by the expansion incident
to a great city, and have, in a measure, lost their peninsular character. No vessel can now approach the an-
chorage from which a British frigate once cannonaded
Charlestown Neck with such destructive effect. The
battle-ground of Breed's Hill is, with the exception of
a small open space about the monument, on its summit,

compactly built upon; still, at Charlestown, enough is remaining to give a clear idea of the battle.

Mr. Froude, on his return to England, mentioned to an American friend, that when at Boston he had not been able to find any one who could tell him the origin of the name of "Bunker," applied to the ever-memorable hill. It would be interesting to know the direction of his research. The name is from George Bunker, an early land-owner in Charlestown; that of Breed having a similar origin.

Boston was commanded on the north and south by the heights of Charlestown and Dorchester peninsulas. The possession of either was sufficient to render it untenable.[1] Generals Howe, Clinton, and Burgoyne, after their arrival in Boston, deemed it indispensable to occupy both positions; and in concert with General Gage, then commanding in chief, had actually planned the seizure of Dorchester Heights on the eighteenth of June, when they were anticipated by the appearance of rebel earthworks on the opposite side of the town. It is credible that the Americans had early intelligence of the intention of the British general, and that the movement on Charlestown was a counter-stroke; if so, it was well conceived, and, so far as depended on the provincial militia, was well executed. With the admission, under the hand of General Burgoyne, that Dorchester Heights were the weak point of the British position, it is inconceivable that they should have remained for ten months afterwards unoccupied, or until Washington opened his batteries there in March, 1776.

---

[1] Dorchester had the more important bearing to the British, as it commanded the inner harbor, and of course covered their shipping; Charlestown was preferred by the Americans, because more accessible from their centre at Cambridge.

If the Americans really meant to offer battle with the hope of deciding the fate of Boston,—and on no other hypothesis can the movement on Charlestown be explained,—it was an exhibition of singular hardihood. They had no officers capable of leading large bodies of troops. They had numbers and courage without discipline or mobility, although they were nominally in regiments and battalions. All their experience of actual service had been gained between the nineteenth of April and the seventeenth of June. As soon as dislodged from their first position on Breed's Hill, they were defeated. Three times the English officers rallied their men under fire, and led them back to the assault. Had the provincials possessed such training, they would easily have won the day, by forming a second line on Bunker Hill: the numbers that moved uselessly about the field were probably more than enough to have decided the battle.

The British remained masters of the ground, and justly claimed the victory. Measured by its results, it was the dearest bought and barrenest victory of the war,— perhaps of any war. The conquerors remained more closely besieged than before. Their losses forbade the execution of any movement to raise the blockade. Their situation was little improved by the fortification of Bunker Hill, and the joy of success was embittered by the reflection that it need not have cost a single life or a charge of gunpowder.

The order to intrench on Bunker Hill was explicit; yet, on arriving there, by the advice of Gridley, the engineer, and probably also of Putnam, Prescott moved on and broke ground at Breed's Hill, a little nearer Boston. It could have made little difference to the English general which hill was fortified. Either commanded Boston on the north and west; and the same reasons that impelled him to attack the one were equally strong with respect to the other. Bunker Hill was the higher of the eminences, but Breed's Hill was by far the best position. It had the town of Charlestown on its right, which might have been filled with troops, and where, in fact, an irregular defence was maintained, until it was burned by the enemy. On its slopes were the stone walls, rail-fences, and orchards, that were used to such terrible purpose. The ground between it and the British landing-place was obstructed by other fences, a morass, and brick-kilns. These natural obstacles were more formidable than the redoubt. They broke the British advance, and in and about the brick-kilns the enemy's loss was particularly severe. The stone and rail-fences, filled between with hay, proved the impregnable point of the American line. The British, after being twice repulsed, and with horrible carnage of the choicest troops on the field, abandoned the effort to carry it. It was the last portion of their line held by the provincials, and covered their retreat.

The mistake of the day appears to have been the omission to throw up some defences on Bunker Hill. Putnam, who seems to have appreciated the importance of a supporting line to raw militia, exerted himself to little purpose for this end. The weak point of the American position was the narrow isthmus over which the troops marched in their advance to and retreat from the peninsula. It was owing to the exhaustion of the British general and army that it did not become the slaughter-pen of the field. The passage of this isthmus, under broadsides from the enemy's shipping, by provincials coming to reinforce their line, is perhaps the remarkable feature of this extraordinary battle.

Had the generalship on the American side equalled
the individual courage, there can be little doubt the
history of Bunker Hill would have had a different read-
ing. General Ward, after launching his offensive blow,
seems to have lacked the energy and decision to follow
it up with the last available man and musket. His blow
was but half delivered. He professed, it is said, to believe his own camp at Cambridge in danger; and, after
having invited a battle, fell back upon the defensive.

The numbers on either side were about equal, and
fluctuated during the day between two and three thousand men. Probably not more than fifteen hundred
Americans manned the lines at any one time during the
engagement. There was much idle marching and coun-
termarching, indecision, and some cowardice behind
them; yet the valor, endurance, and heroic constancy
of that day have never been surpassed since arms were
first borne by men.

At the time of the battle, the British force in Boston
consisted of the following regiments and parts of regiments, besides six companies of royal artillery and
two battalions of marines; the whole numbering, probably, six thousand effective men. Some of these corps
were the very *élite* of the army. These were the 4th,
or Hodgson's (King's Own); 5th, Percy's; 10th, Sand-
ford's; 18th, or Royal Irish (three companies); 22d,
Gage's; 23d, Howe's (Welsh Fusileers); 35th, F. H.
Campbell's; 38th, Pigot's; 43d, cary's (Monmouth-
shire Light Infantry); 47th, Carleton's; 52d, Clavering's (Oxfordshire Light Infantry); 63d, Grant's; 65th,
Urmston's (two companies). The marching regiments
for the American service consisted of twelve companies,
and each company mustered fifty-six effective rank and
file. Two companies of each regiment were usually left
at home on recruiting service.

These troops were in barracks or intrenched camps on Boston Common, the Neck communicating with the mainland, Fort Hill on the east, Copp's Hill on the north, and Beacon Hill on the west, of the town. A battery had been erected on Copp's Hill, commanding Charlestown, and strong works had also been carried across the Neck in the vicinity of where are now Dedham and Canton Streets. No troops, except, perhaps, those of Frederick the Great, could dispute the claim of the British infantry of that day to be considered the first in Europe, and the regiments now serving in Boston were the choicest troops that army could muster.

The general organization and *morale* of the provincial forces have been touched upon. The headquarters were at Cambridge, with a corps under General John Thomas, cantoned at Roxbury, in order to observe the enemy, or check an advance by land. General Ward held the nominal command, but all operations were directed by a junto called the Committee of Safety, whose orders were final. Some defensive works had been begun in the American centre, and towards their left.

It is not believed that any flag was displayed by the provincial forces at Bunker Hill. No British account of the battle mentions any; and yet it would have been the first thing to which the attention of a soldier would have been directed. If a British color had been seen flying within the American lines, the fact would have been little likely to escape remark; and if any other flag had been flying there, its peculiarity would have attracted the curious observation of the whole British army. It is safe, therefore, in the absence of direct proof to the contrary, to declare that no flag was unfurled by the Americans on that day, and that the "Star Banner" of Mr. Carlyle yet hung high in the heavens.

The representation of the battle in the *frontispiece* is a heliotype reproduction of a very rare English print, published in London in 1781. The accuracy of some of its details may be questioned, and the configuration of the battle-ground is suggestive of Gibraltar, rather than Bunker Hill. Its general features, however, betray a tolerably authentic paternity, and it may have been copied from some rough sketch made on the spot.

The narrative of the battle by "John Clarke," who styles himself "first lieutenant of marines," has been quoted, but is now given in full, and as an appropriate pendant to the other British accounts. It is not indorsed as authority.[1] The accounts of Lord Harris, and General Burgoyne's letter to Lord Stanley, are now also printed in full, as the relations of eye-witnesses.

---

[1] No such name appears in the roster of the marine battalions, as given in their records; nor in the list of promotions after the battle. Other inaccuracies render it doubtful if Clarke served in the horse or foot. His narrative possesses, however, a curious interest, as a production of the same year with the battle.

The second edition, which is given in the text, was printed in London in 1775, and is entitled "An Impartial and Authentic Narrative of the Battle fought on the 17th of June, 1775, between His Britannic Majesty's Troops and the American Provincial Army, on Bunker's Hill, near Charlestown, in New England." It is the only account containing the address of Howe to his troops.

CHAPTER I

THE BATTLE

THE BATTLE.

O N the morning of the 17th of June, 1775, the inhabitants and garrison of Boston were aroused by a heavy cannonade. The cause of the firing was soon apparent. A large body of provincial militia was plainly seen, from the house-tops and eminences of Boston, busily at work intrenching on Breed's Hill, in Charlestown. This discovery had first been made at daybreak, from the ships of war lying in the stream, one of which had opened her batteries upon the adventurous workmen. The firing was soon augmented by the broadsides of other ships, and by a battery of field guns on Copp's Hill, the nearest point to the hostile works on the Boston side of Charles River. The Americans, however, pursued their labor with unremitting diligence, regardless of the shower of cannon-shot directed against them.

General Gage immediately called the superior officers of his troops together, in council. It was agreed that the Americans must be expelled from their position, but a discussion of the proper plan of attack elicited two conflicting opinions. Some of the officers[1] approved of landing at Charlestown Neck, seizing the communica-

[1] General Clinton among others; and, by implication, Howe and Burgoyne, as the latter says, in his account of the battle, he and his colleagues never differed an iota in the military plans.

tion between the provincials and their main body, and taking their works in reverse. General Gage, for various reasons, preferred an attack in front, and orders were issued to prepare for it. Ten companies of light infantry, ten of grenadiers, the 5th, 38th, 43d, and 52d regiments, and some companies of the royal artillery, were ordered under arms. Twelve pieces of artillery were to accompany the attacking force, which a very moderate estimate fixes at two thousand men.[1] General Howe, next in rank to General Gage, was ordered to take the command.

These troops embarked about noon in two divisions, protected by a tremendous fire from the shipping, and landed without opposition at Moulton's (or Morton's) Point, near the head of the present Chelsea Bridge. Many an eye that glanced curiously at the embankments crowning the heights above them, before nightfall was glazed in death. Bouillon and Collingwood, of subsequent naval renown, were in the boats, assisting in transporting the troops.

General Howe formed his troops where he landed, in three lines, each having a front of two regiments: the grenadiers and light infantry occupied the first, the 38th and 5th the second, the 52d and 43d the third line, counting from left to right; the artillery was posted in front. Howe then reconnoitred, and, obtaining a juster idea of the strength of the American position, caused his troops to rest and eat their dinners on the ground where they stood, while he sent back to Boston a request for reinforcements. The Americans continued to ply the

[1] The regiments engaged should be counted as having only eight companies, the two flank companies of each being included with the twenty of light infantry and grenadiers, on the field. The companies did not, probably, average forty men fit for duty.

spade until the British had landed, when they laid aside their intrenching tools and prepared for the coming conflict.

Since midnight of the sixteenth, the Americans had thrown up a redoubt of about eight rods square, and an embankment on its left flank, extending about a hundred yards toward the Mystic. This work had been performed by a thousand Massachusetts and Connecticut men, commanded by Colonel William Prescott. Exhausted by the incessant toil of nearly twelve hours, these men, nevertheless, under the example of their indomitable leader, endured to the end the greater ordeal of the battle.

Before the action began, the Americans completed their line to the Mystic by occupying a low stone-wall, having wooden rails above, situated near the base of Bunker Hill, and two hundred yards in rear of the redoubt. This protection they strengthened with the rails of other fences, heaping the space between with the new-mown hay then lying in mounds on the field. The Connecticut militia under Knowlton, and New Hampshire troops of Stark and Reed, with some Massachusetts men, defended this rustic breastwork with equal gallantry and success. They had here two light six-pounders, which made terrible practice later in the day. The American front was now substantially complete, except in the interval between the breastwork and the stone-wall, which was occupied by such slight natural obstacles as trees and fences, but presented a wide gap in the line. The line was also prolonged on the right of the redoubt by defences similar to those improvised on the left.

Both sides were reinforced before the battle began in earnest. Colonels Stark and Reed had come on the field with their New Hampshire regiments, and had taken post at the fence, on the left. Some other detachments had also joined, and General Warren, whose presence animated the Americans with new courage, came to announce the speedy arrival of other reinforcements. At Putnam's suggestion he chose the redoubt as the post of honor, and having, on entering it, been offered the command by Prescott, declined it, saying, he came to act the part of a good soldier. Pomeroy, another general officer, also reached the ground, and took his station at the rail-fence. Putnam was there and everywhere, making the efforts of a Hercules to ensure the success of the day. Frye and Nixon and Gridley had seen service at Louisburg, and knew what fighting meant.

Howe's request had been promptly answered by sending him the 47th regiment, the first marine battalion, and some additional companies of light-infantry and grenadiers. These troops landed near the present entrance to the Navy Yard, and acted under the orders of Colonel Nesbitt of the 47th. Pitcairn led his marines. It was now three in the afternoon, and both combatants were as ready as they were likely to be.

The British artillery was ordered to begin, while Howe deployed his troops in columns of attack. The light-infantry moved by the right along the beach of Mystic River. It was ordered to turn the rail-fence and clear the ground behind it. The grenadiers marched directly for the rail-fence to support this attack, which General Howe personally superintended. The left attack was formed of all the other regiments enumerated, advancing in line along the American front, directing their march upon the breastwork and redoubt. General Pigot commanded this division. Howe expected to break through the American left and assail from their rear the troops in the redoubt and breastwork. If he succeeded, he was in a position to intercept the Americans' line of retreat, and to envelop them with his right.[1] He calculated on an easy victory; but the rail-fence was never taken until the loss of the redoubt and breastwork rendered it untenable.

The British guns advanced and opened fire at about half-past three o'clock, followed by the troops, who moved slowly forward, and occasionally halted, in order to allow the artillery to make some impression. The day was very fine and very warm, and the attacking columns were encumbered with full marching equipments. They had occasionally to pull down fences in their way, and the grass, high and fit for mowing, also impeded them. In the soft ground, in the neighborhood of the brick-kilns, some of the guns became unable to advance, and were halted. British accounts say their troops received here a very destructive fire.

Arriving within musket-shot of the American works, the troops commenced firing, receiving in return only a few scattering shots, until they came within about seventy yards. The provincials had been ordered all along their line to reserve their fire until they could see the white of their enemies' eyes. The troops, though doubting what this ominous silence might mean, continued to sweep the ramparts with their musketry, and to advance. When the English battle-line crossed the fatal boundary, already determined, a sonorous voice within the redoubt cried out, "Fire!"

[1] Burgoyne pronounced Howe's dispositions perfect; other British authorities considered them faulty. Had he succeeded in breaking through the American line at the rail-fence, the provincials would have been obliged to fight in the open field, or retreat at great disadvantage, with the enemy between them and Bunker Hill. The British commander's error was more in his tactics than the plan of battle.

Then began that terrible fusilade, which so many have in vain attempted to describe. A blaze ran along the whole line; the hill shook. Like the leap of a pent-up wave of fire from out a burning building, it rolled and surged down upon the English line, bursting through and overwhelming it,—flashing with deadly gleams, and crested with battle-smoke. Whole companies withered away. Standards sunk out of sight, and ranks of muskets fell from nerveless hands. When it had passed, a broken line of bewildered men, unable to advance, unwilling to fly, stood where the heaps of the dead and dying were more than the groups of the living. Then the bugles sounded the recall, and they retreated to the shore, where the Americans' exultant hurrah followed them.

Both divisions were repulsed by the same tactics,— the same cool waiting for the command which allowed deliberate and accurate aim. Every muzzle pointed to its victim minutes before the order was given to fire.

British valor could not endure defeat, and Howe, gathering his columns together, resolved on a second effort. Charlestown had afforded some cover to provincial marksmen, and was set on fire. The Americans, who had thus far suffered little loss, were exasperated by the sight. Their countrymen were anxiously watching them from every house-top and hill-side that commanded a view of the field. The roar of cannon, the musket volleys, the crackling of flames, and the swathes of thick smoke, hanging above, made every combatant an actor in a theatre such as few lifetimes have witnessed.

The British repeated the same manœuvre, and with the same result as before, except that the troops were more dispirited at their want of success, more shaken by the appalling slaughter. This was not fighting, they said, but downright butchery. Many valuable officers had fallen, and with them a third of the numbers that had first obeyed the order to advance. The desperate situation of affairs was perceived in Boston. A second reinforcement of marines was sent to Howe, and General Clinton, with the impulse of a gallant soldier, crossed the river in a boat and placed himself at the head of some broken battalions to take part in the closing scene. This was the critical moment of the day.

For the third time Howe succeeded in rallying and forming his gallant little army. The knowledge gained in the previous attacks was now used to advantage. The men threw off their knapsacks and the officers their blankets. The artillery was ordered to take a position to enfilade the fatal gap between the breastwork and rail-fence. Howe placed himself at the head of the light infantry and grenadiers, and marched against the breastwork. Clinton and Pigot led their columns against the redoubt. The soldiers were ordered to move at a quick step, and use the bayonet only.

The British artillery soon drove the defenders of the breastwork into the redoubt. Powder had become scarce; yet the provincials awaited with the same calmness as before the expected onset. One deadly volley shot in pieces the head of the British column, and staggered it; but it pressed on to the wall of the work, flowed over the rampart, and closed in hand-to-hand encounter with the brave garrison. The day was lost, though the Americans still contested it in their retreat. Warren was killed and left on the field. Putnam and Prescott and Pomeroy and Stark sullenly gave ground and retired as the enemy advanced. Howe, having now won the peninsula, brought one of his shattered regi-

ments to the front, where it bivouacked. Other troops
passed the weary night lying on their arms, or throwing up intrenchments on Bunker Hill. A thousand
and more of the flower of English soldiery lay dead or
wounded in front of the American lines.

At five o'clock the battle was over. The Americans,
though beaten from the peninsula, took a more advanced
position than any they had yet occupied. They lost over
four hundred in killed and wounded, but had met and
disputed in regular battle with troops who, until then,
believed themselves invincible. They also lost five of
the six small field guns which they took into action.
From this day the head of a British column was never
seen on the shore of the mainland, and the contest for
the possession of Boston was reduced to a question of
artillery practice.

CHAPTER II

THE SHARE OF THE 4TH

OR KING'S OWN REGIMENT

II.

THE SHARE OF THE 4TH, OR KING'S OWN, REGIMENT.[1]

———

DURING the night of the 16th of June an immense body of provincials proceeded to the heights on the peninsula of Charlestown, called Bunker's Hill, and commenced throwing up intrenchments with great diligence. General Gage resolved to dislodge the enemy from this post immediately; and a body of troops, of which the grenadier and light companies of the "King's Own" formed part, was embarked in boats for this purpose about mid-day on the 17th of June.

About three o'clock in the afternoon the attack commenced, and in this contest British valor and discipline were eminently displayed. The Americans were in great force, strongly posted, and intrenched up to the teeth. The king's troops had to advance in a hot summer's day, in the face of a sharp and well-directed fire, and to ascend a steep hill covered with grass reaching to their knees, and intersected with walls and fences of various enclosures. Twice they were stopped, and twice they returned to the charge; and by their undaunted resolution and steady perseverance they eventually triumphed over thrice their own numbers, and carried the heights at the point of the bayonet. This proved one of the most sanguinary battles on record, and the superiority of the British troops was pre-eminently displayed. The two flank companies of the King's Own had

[1] "Historical Record of the 4th Regiment of Foot."

one serjeant and thirteen rank and file killed; Captains Balfour and West, Lieutenants Baron and Brown, one serjeant, one drummer, and twenty-nine rank and file wounded.[1]

[1] This regiment has a remarkable record. It has fought in Africa, Ireland, the Netherlands, Spain, Canada (1711), Scotland, Belgium, Havana (1762); the American War, from Lexington until 1778; the West Indies, Nova Scotia, Holland, Sweden, Denmark, the Peninsular War, and second war with America (1812.) It was at the taking of Washington, and at New Orleans it lost nearly four hundred men. The regiment was twice at Boston,—first in 1711, under Colonel Seymour. Charles, Earl of Plymouth, a natural son of Charles II., was first colonel; Piercy Kirke (Jeffrey's executioner) also commanded it; Studholme Hodgson was colonel, 1768 to 1782, then John Burgoyne; and in the War of 1812, John, Earl of Chatham.

CHAPTER III

RECORD OF THE 52D
OXFORDSHIRE LIGHT INFANTRY

III.

RECORD OF THE 52D, OXFORDSHIRE LIGHT INFANTRY.

THE Americans were plainly seen at work throwing up intrenchments around the hill, and preparations were at once made for landing a body of men to dislodge the enemy and take possession of the works. Ten companies of grenadiers, ten of light-infantry, with the 5th, 38th, 43d, and 52d regiments, with a proportion of field artillery, were detailed for this service.

Embarking from Boston in boats about noon on the 17th of June, the troops crossed the river, and landed on the opposite shore, where they formed immediately; the light-infantry being posted on the right, and the grenadiers upon their left. The 5th and 38th drew up in the rear of those corps, and the 43d and 52d formed a third line. The ships of war opened their fire upon the enemy's works, and the troops ascended the steep hill and advanced to storm the intrenchments. The approach to the hill was covered with grass reaching to the knees, and intersected with walls and fences of various enclosures. The difficult ascent, the heat of the weather, and the superior numbers of the enemy, together with their accurate and incessant fire, made the enterprise particularly arduous. The light-infantry were directed to force the left point of the breastwork, to take the enemy's line in flank, while the grenadiers were to attack in front, supported by the 5th and 52d regiments. These orders were executed with perseverance, and, notwithstanding the numerous impediments offered, the enemy was forced from his stronghold and driven from the peninsula, leaving behind five pieces of cannon.

4

In this action the 52d particularly distinguished itself. It suffered, however, severely; the whole of the grenadier company were either killed or wounded.

The late General Martin Hunter, who was present as an ensign in the 52d, writes in his journal: "The grenadiers and light companies (of the several regiments before enumerated) attacked the breastworks extending from the Charlestown Heights (or Bunker Hill) redoubt to the Mystic River, while the remaining companies attacked the redoubt itself. About one hundred yards from the latter they were stopped by some brick-kilns and enclosures, and exposed for some time to the whole of its fire; and it was here that so many men were lost. The remains of the 52d regiment continued at the advanced post the whole of the night after the battle; several attacks were made on them during the night, but the Americans were constantly repulsed."

The following is the official return of killed and wounded on this occasion: Captains Nicholas Addison, George Amos Smith, and William Davison, one serjeant, and twenty rank and file, were killed. Major Arthur Williams, who was specially noticed in the dispatch from General Gage, did not survive his wounds. Captain-lieutenant Andrew Neilson, Lieutenants Henry Crawfurd, John Thompson, and Robert Harpur Higgins, Ensigns the Honorable William Chetwynd,——Graeme, and volunteer Robert John Harrison, and seven serjeants and seventy-three rank and file, were wounded. Lieutenant Higgins died on the 24th of June.[1]

---

[1] The annals of this regiment present some interesting souvenirs of the war. The 52d was afterwards in the attack on Fort Washington (Hudson River). General Martin Hunter, who was present, says in his journal: "The light-infantry embarked at King's Bridge in flat-bottomed boats, and proceeded up the East River (?) under a very heavy cannonade. They landed, and stormed a battery, and afterwards took possession of a hill that commanded the fort (Washington). Before landing, the fire of cannon and musketry was so heavy that the sailors quitted their oars and lay down in the bottom of the boats; and had not the soldiers taken the oars and pulled on shore, we must have remained in this situation." The 52d was engaged at Rhode Island, and in the massacre of Wayne's corps. It was the first battalion attacked at Germantown. When retreating before the furious onset

of Washington, General Howe came to the front and reproached the corps with much passion: "For shame, light-infantry! I never saw you retreat before: form! form! it's only a scouting party." A shower of grape from the American cannon having fallen among the crowd that were standing with the general, he rode off at full speed from the "scouting party," to the huge enjoyment of the veterans he had just accused of cowardice.

At Monmouth, Powell, the fourth captain of the grenadier company killed during the war, having fallen, the drummer of his company was heard to exclaim, "Well, I wonder who they'll get to accept of our grenadier company now? I'll be d—d if I would!"

In 1778, the regiment, being reduced to ninety-two effective men, was sent home to England. It had been raised in 1755 (Seven Years' War), and was first numbered 54th; but on account of the disbandment of Colonel Shirley's and Sir William Pepperell's regiments (50th and 51st), it became the 52d. Sir John Clavering was its colonel during the American War; Sir John Moore and Lieutenant-general Martin Hunter had been lieutenants; Field-marshal Lord Seaton commanded it in 1812. At Bunker Hill the 52d and 43d began that soldierly brotherhood afterwards cemented on the famous fields of the Peninsular War.

CHAPTER IV

ACCOUNT OF ADJUTANT WALLER
ROYAL MARINES

IV.

ACCOUNT OF ADJUTANT WALLER, ROYAL MARINES.

CAMP OF CHARLESTOWN HEIGHTS, 22d June, 1775.

MY DEAR BROTHER,—Amidst the hurry and confusion of a camp hastily pitched in the field of battle, I am sat down to tell you I have escaped unhurt, where many, very many, have fallen. The public papers will inform you of the situation of the ground and the redoubt that we attacked on the heights of Charlestown. I can only say that it was a most desperate and daring attempt, and it was performed with as much gallantry and spirit as was ever shown by any troops in any age.

Two companies of the first battalion of marines, and part of the 47th regiment, were the first that mounted the breastwork; and you will not be displeased when I tell you that I was with those two companies who drove their bayonets into all that opposed them. Nothing could be more shocking than the carnage that followed the storming this work. We tumbled over the dead to get at the living, who were crowding out of the gorge of the redoubt, in order to form under the defences which they had prepared to cover their retreat. In these breastworks they had artillery, which did so much mischief; but these they were obliged to abandon, being followed closely by the light-infantry, who suffered exceedingly in the pursuit. The rebels had five thousand to seven thousand men, covered by a redoubt, breastworks, walls, hedges, trees, and the like; and the number of the corps under General Howe (who performed this gallant business) did not amount to fifteen hundred. We gained a complete victory, and intrenched ourselves that night, where we lay under arms, in the front of the field of battle. We lay the next night on the ground, and the following day encamped. The officers have not their marquees, but are obliged to lie in soldiers' tents, they being more portable in case of our advancing.

We had of our corps one major, two captains, and three lieutenants killed; four captains and three lieutenants wounded; two serjeants, and twenty-one rank and file killed; and three serjeants and seventy-nine privates wounded; and, I suppose, upon the whole, we lost, killed and wounded, from eight hundred to one thousand men. We killed a number of the rebels, but the cover they fought under made their loss less considerable than it would otherwise have been. The army is in great spirits, and full of rage and ferocity at the rebellious rascals who both poisoned and chewed the musket-balls, in order to make them the more fatal. Many officers have died of their wounds, and others very ill; 'tis astonishing what a number of officers were hit on this occasion: but the officers were particularly aimed at.

I will just give you a short account of the part of the action where I was particularly concerned. We landed close under Charlestown, and formed with the 47th regiment close under the natural defences of the redoubt, which we drove the enemy from, climbing over rails and hedges. So we closed upon them; but when we came immediately under the work, we were checked by the severe fire of the enemy, but did not retreat an inch. We were now in confusion, after being broke several times in getting over the rails, &c. I did all I could to form the two companies on our right, which at last I effected, losing many of them while it was performing. Major Pitcairne was killed close by me, with a captain and a subaltern, also a sergeant, and many of the privates; and had we stopped there much longer, the enemy would have picked us all off. I saw this, and begged Colonel Nesbitt, of the 47th, to form on our left, in order that we might advance with our bayonets to the parapet. I ran from right to left, and stopped our men from firing; while this was doing, and when we had got in tolerable order, we rushed on, leaped the

ditch, and climbed the parapet, under a most sore and heavy
fire. Colonel Nesbitt has spoken very favorably of my con-
duct, and both our majors have mentioned me to Lord Sand-
wich in consequence of it. One captain and one subaltern
fell in getting up, and one captain and one subaltern were
wounded of our corps; three captains of the 52d were killed
on the parapet, and others that I know nothing of. God bless
you! I did not think, at one time, that I should ever have
been able to write this, though in the heat of the action I
thought nothing of the matter.

Adieu, dear Jacob, yours,

J. WALLER.

CHAPTER V

ROYAL MARINES

V.

THE ROYAL MARINES.

O N the 8th of June the American congress resolved "that the compact between the crown and the people of Massachusetts Bay is dissolved." A proclamation was issued by General Gage establishing martial law, and offering pardon to all who should return to their allegiance, excepting Samuel Adams and John Handcock. Matters were thus fast approaching to a crisis, and both parties prepared in right earnest for the struggle.

At this moment, the town of Charlestown was not occupied by either party; and the rebels, anticipating the movement of the king's troops, sent a large body of men on the 16th of June to erect works upon Bunker's Hill; and during the night they raised intrenchments, and constructed a formidable redoubt. On the 17th, at daybreak, the garrison of Boston was alarmed by a heavy cannonade from his Majesty's ship "Lively," directed against the working party on the hill; but as the Americans persevered in their labors with great firmness, General Gage considered it highly necessary to dislodge them from so important a position, and therefore resolved on an immediate attack.

The "Lively," "Falcon," and "Spitfire" having anchored abreast of and below Charlestown for covering the landing of the troops, at nine in the morning the "Glasgow," lying off New Point, and a battery of six guns and some howitzers, opened upon the rebels; but they perseveringly continued their work, nothing daunted by the heavy fire which was poured upon them. The Americans on the heights were in great force, and strongly posted in a redoubt, besides other works, on which they had mounted cannon. In the houses of Charlestown, which covered their right flank, they had also posted a large body of troops, while their centre and left flank were protected by a breastwork, partly cannon proof: and these works reached from the left of the redoubt to the Mystic, or Medford River. Ten companies of grenadiers and ten of light-infantry, with the 5th, 38th, 43d, and 52d regiments, under Major-general Howe and Brigadier-general Pigot, were embarked with great expedition, and landed about noon on Charlestown Point, under the protection of the ships of war, whose well-directed fire kept the insurgents within their works. The troops formed in perfect order, the light-infantry under Brigadier Pigot posted on the right, and the grenadiers on the left; in rear of these the 5th and 38th regiments, and the 43d and 52d in a third line. Major-general Howe, on examining the state of the enemy's defences, and observing fresh columns pouring in to their assistance, solicited a reinforcement, which soon joined him, consisting of some companies of grenadiers and light-infantry, the 47th regiment, and the battalions of marines, who were led by Majors Pitcairne, Tupper, and Short. The major-general then formed the corps under his command into two lines, and immediately advanced towards the enemy's works. About half-past three o'clock a smart fire was opened from the field-pieces and howitzers of the British, as the troops slowly advanced, and occasionally halting to allow the artillery to fire with greater effect. The light-infantry was directed to force the left point of the breastwork, and take the enemy in flank; whilst the grenadiers were to attack in front, supported by the 5th and 52d regiments. Not a shot was returned by the enemy until our troops were close upon them, when they opened a destructive fire, which was so well maintained that it somewhat staggered the assailants. For some time the British withstood this opposition; but their loss of officers and men was so great that they recoiled a little, and fell into disorder, until the animating presence of General Howe restored confidence, when the soldiers rallied, and again advanced upon the enemy.

At this time the left wing, from being much exposed to the enemy's fire from the houses of Charlestown, sustained considerable loss; orders were therefore sent to destroy the place, which was speedily effected by red-hot shot from the ships, and by Cape's (Copp's) Hill battery throwing carcasses. General Howe now renewed his attack; and, overcoming the various impediments thrown in their way, the British soldiers rushed into the intrenchments with the bayonet, and drove the gallant enemy from every part of the works across the peninsula, leaving five pieces of cannon in our possession. At the commencement of the action the rebels had above five thousand men, and their loss must have been considerable; but only thirty of the killed remained in the redoubt. In this hardly-earned victory the loss on the part of the British amounted to one lieutenant-colonel, two majors, seven captains, nine lieutenants, fifteen serjeants, one drummer, and one hundred and ninety-one rank and file, killed; three majors, twenty-seven captains, thirty-two lieutenants, eight ensigns, and seven hundred and fifty-eight privates, wounded,—making a total of ten hundred and fifty-four in killed and wounded.

The marine battalions sustained more than its proportionate share of casualties:—

First battalion: Major Short, Captain Stephen Ellis, Lieutenants Richard Shea and William Finnie, and seventeen men, killed. Major Pitcairne, mortally; Captains Thomas Avarne, Stawel Chudleigh, and David Johnstone, Lieutenant Ragg, and fifty-seven men, wounded.

Second battalion: Captain Archibald Campbell, Lieutenant Francis Gardner, and five men, killed; Captain George Logan, Lieutenants John Dyer, Alexander Brisbane, and thirty men, wounded.

The reputation of the marines was never more nobly sustained than in this sanguinary contest. Their unshaken firmness was conspicuous, and the valor they displayed in closing with the enemy, when some part of the attacking column wavered, gained them not only the admiration of their comrades, but the commendation of their distinguished chief.

5

General Orders, 19 *June,* 1775.

The Commander-in-chief returns his most grateful thanks to Major-general Howe for the extraordinary exertion of his military abilities on the 17th instant. He returns his thanks also to Major-general Clinton and Brigadier Pigot for the share they took in the success of the day, as well as to Lieutenant-colonels Nesbitt, Abercromby, Gunning, and Clarke, Majors Butler, Williams, Bruce, Tupper, Spenlove, Small, and Mitchel, and the rest of the officers and soldiers, who by remarkable efforts of courage and gallantry overcame every disadvantage, and drove the rebels from the redoubt and strongholds on the heights of Charlestown, and gained a complete victory.[1]

---

[1] "Historical Record Royal Marine Forces."

CHAPTER VI

THE ROYAL ARTILLERY AT BUNKER HILL

VI.

THE ROYAL ARTILLERY AT BUNKER HILL.

O N the 17th of June, 1775, the Battle of Bunker's Hill, as it is called, although Breed's Hill was the real scene of operations (Bunker's Hill, which was intended to be fortified, being considerably more distant from Boston), was fought; and between the batteries on Cop's Hill, and with the guns actually on the field, five companies of the fourth battalion were present, Nos. 1, 2, 4, 5, and 8. Eight field guns were actually in action; but twelve accompanied the attacking force,—four light twelve-pounders, four 5½-inch howitzers, and four light six-pounders. The attack was made under the fire of the guns, "the troops advancing slowly, and halting at intervals to give time for the artillery to produce some effect." In these words the recently exploded traditions are apparent which wedded the artillery to the infantry during an engagement, instead of allowing it independent action. One statement is made by Stedman, generally a most accurate writer, which it is difficult to reconcile with Colonel Cleaveland's official report. "During the engagement," writes the former, "a supply of ball for the artillery, sent from the ordnance department in Boston, was found to be of larger dimensions than fitted the calibres of the field-pieces that accompanied the detachment, an oversight which prevented the further use of the artillery."

In opposition to this statement, Colonel Cleaveland's report to the Master-general may be quoted: "At Bunker's Hill I sent sixty-six rounds to each gun, and not more than half was fired." The artillery met with but little casualty. According to the Fourth Battalion records, Captain-lieutenant Lemoine, Lieutenant Shuttleworth, and nine matrosses were wounded; according to Colonel Cleaveland's MSS, this number was increased by Captain Huddlestone, whom he includes among the wounded.

The English plan of attack was faulty, and the defence of the Americans admirable; but these facts merely rendered the victory of the English troops more creditable. It did not save Boston from the blockade, which from this day became more thorough; and it certainly encouraged the American militia, who found with what effect they could fight against those regular troops from which they had hitherto shrunk a little, with a species of superstitious dread.[1]

[1] "History Royal Artillery."

CHAPTER VII

ACCOUNT OF CAPTAIN HARRIS
OF THE 5TH FOOT

VII.

ACCOUNT OF CAPTAIN HARRIS,[1] OF THE 5TH FOOT.

————

W E had made a breach in their fortifications, which I had twice mounted, encouraging the men to follow me, and was ascending a third time, when a ball grazed the top of my head, and I fell, deprived of sense and motion. My lieutenant, Lord Rawdon, caught me in his arms, and, believing me dead, endeavored to remove me from the spot, to save my body from being trampled on. The motion, while it hurt me, restored my senses, and I articulated, "For God's sake, let me die in peace."

The hope of preserving my life induced Lord Rawdon to order four soldiers to take me up, and carry me to a place of safety. Three of them were wounded while performing this office (one afterwards died of his wounds); but they succeeded in placing me under some trees out of the reach of the balls. A retreat having been sounded, poor Holmes was running about like a madman in search of me, and luckily came to the place where I lay, just in time to prevent my being left behind, for when they brought me to the water's edge, the last boat was put off, the men calling out "they would take no more!" On Holmes' hallooing out, "It is Captain Harris," they put back

————

[1] Afterward George, Lord Harris. He commanded the grenadier company, his lieutenant being Lord Rawdon, subsequently Marquis of Hastings. Harris served in America, in the West Indies, and in the East Indies. He commanded as lieutenant-general the army which captured Seringapatam, in which Tippoo Sultan was killed. After Bunker Hill his life was saved by trepanning. He notes that his surgeons, by fixing looking-glasses, gratified him with a view of his own brains,—Diary of Lord Harris, in his "Life and Services." London, 1845.

and took me in. I was very weak and faint, and seized with a severe shivering. Our blankets had been flung away during the engagement; luckily there was one belonging to a man in the boat, in which, wrapping me up, and laying me in the bottom, they conveyed me safely to my quarters.[1]

[1] Captain Harris was with his company in the Battle of Lexington and Concord. Lord Percy, his colonel, placed him in command of the rear guard on the retreat, as Colonel Smith had given the advance to one of the 10th in the march to Concord. Harris's company was, as he himself relates, very roughly handled. Captain Parsons, of the 10th, who also figured prominently at Concord, was among the wounded at Bunker Hill.

CHAPTER VIII

GENERAL BURGOYNE'S LETTER TO LORD STANLEY

VIII.

GENERAL BURGOYNE'S LETTER TO LORD STANLEY.[1]

BOSTON is a peninsula, joined to the mainland only by a narrow neck, which, on the first troubles, General Gage fortified; arms of the sea and the harbor form the rest; on the other side of one of these arms, to the north, is Charlestown (or rather was, for it is now rubbish), and over it a large hill, which is also, like Boston, a peninsula. To the south of the town is a still larger scope of ground, containing three hills, joining also to the mainland by a tongue, and called Dorchester Neck, the neck above described; both north and south (in the soldier phrase) commanded the town, that is, gave an opportunity of erecting batteries above any we can make against them, and consequently are much more advantageous. It was absolutely necessary we should make ourselves masters of these heights, and we proposed to begin with Dorchester, because, from the particular situation of the batteries and shipping, it would evidently be effected without any considerable loss. Every thing was disposed accordingly. My two colleagues and myself (who, by the by, have never differed in one jot of military sentiment) had, in concert with General Gage, formed the plan. Howe was to land the transports on one point, Clinton in the centre, and I was to cannonade from the causeway, or the neck, each to take advantage of the circumstances. The operations must have been very easy. This was to have been executed on the

---

[1] General Burgoyne witnessed the battle from Copp's Hill. He and Lord Percy remained on duty in Boston; the former cannonaded General Thomas at Roxbury from the British lines on Boston Neck, in order to prevent reinforcements being despatched to the battle-field.

18th. On the 17th, at dawn of day, we found the enemy had
pushed intrenchments with great diligence during the night
on the heights of Charlestown, and we evidently saw that every
hour gave them fresh strength; it therefore became necessary
to alter our plan, and attack on that side. Howe, as second in
command, was detached with about two thousand men, and
landed on the outward side of the peninsula, covered with shipping, without opposition. He was to advance from thence up
the hill, which was over Charlestown, where the strength of
the enemy lay. He had under him Brigadier-general Pigot.
Clinton and myself took our stand (for we had not any fixed
post) in a large battery opposite to Charlestown, and commanding it, and also reaching to the height above it, and thereby
facilitating Howe's attack. Howe's disposition was extremely
soldier-like: in my opinion, it was perfect. As his first arm
advanced up, they met with a thousand impediments from
strong fences, and were much exposed. They were also very
much hurt by the musketry from Charlestown, though Clinton
and I did not perceive it, till Howe sent us word by a boat, and
desired us to set fire to the town, which was immediately done.
We threw a parcel of shells, and the whole was instantly in
flames. Our battery afterwards kept an incessant fire on the
heights; it was seconded by a number of frigates, floating-
batteries, and one ship of the line.

And now ensued one of the greatest scenes of war that can
be conceived, if we look to the height. Howe's corps, ascending the hill in the face of intrenchments, and in a very
disadvantageous ground, was much engaged; and to the left, the
enemy pouring in fresh troops by thousands over the land;
and in the arm of the sea, our ships and floating batteries cannonading them; straight before us, a large and noble town in
one blaze: the church-steeples, being made of timber, were
great pyramids of fire above the rest; behind us, the church-
steeples and heights of our camp covered with spectators. The
enemy all anxious suspense; the roar of cannon, mortars,
musketry; the crash of churches, ships upon the stocks, and
whole streets falling together in ruin, to fill the ear; the storm
of the redoubts, with the objects above described, to fill the

eye; and the reflection, that, perhaps, a defeat was a final loss to the British Empire in America, to fill the mind,—made the whole a picture, and complication of horror and importance, beyond any thing that came to my lot to be a witness to. I much lament my nephew's absence: it was a sight for a young soldier that the longest service may not furnish again; and had he been with me he would likewise have been out of danger, for except two cannon-balls that went a hundred yards over our heads, we were not in any part of the direction of the enemy's shot. A moment of the day was critical. Howe's left was staggered; two battalions had been sent to reinforce them, but we perceived them on a beach, seeming in embarrassment which way to march. Clinton, then next for business, took the part, without waiting for orders, to throw himself into a boat to lead them; he arrived in time to be of service. The day ended with glory, and the success was most important, considering the ascendancy it gives the regular troops; but the loss was uncommon among the officers, considering the numbers engaged.

CHAPTER IX

AN AUTHENTIC AND IMPARTIAL NARRATIVE OF THE BATTLE FOUGHT ON THE 17TH OF JUNE, 1775

IX.

AN AUTHENTIC AND IMPARTIAL NARRATIVE OF THE
BATTLE FOUGHT ON THE 17TH OF JUNE, 1775, &c.[1]

O N Friday, the sixteenth of June, 1775, Lieutenant-general
Gage, Commander-in-chief of all his Majesty's troops in
America, and Governor of Boston, received information that the
provincial American army were erecting a battery on Bunker's
Hill, contiguous to Charlestown, with an intent to besiege and
annoy the town of Boston. This information was soon confirmed by their firing several cannon-balls into the town, to
the infinite terror and danger of the inhabitants, most of whom
then within the town were in general deemed and esteemed
the steady friends of government.

In consequence of this insult to his Majesty's troops and
government, Lieutenant-general Gage thought it expedient to
give orders for the men-of-war, transports, &c., and the military,
to make every necessary preparation for an action.

On the subsequent day, Saturday, the 17th of June, in com-
pliance with these orders, every necessary disposal from the
fleet and army was made by ten in the morning, and such
troops as were ordered upon the expedition were embarked at
Hancock's Wharf, and effected their landing under the cover of
the shipping by one.

Two transports, also with troops, arrived from England the
night before, were ordered to land in the morning on Charlestown side to proceed to the engagement.

Immediately after landing, Major-general Howe, Major Pitcairn, and other principal officers, directly drew up the troops
to the best advantage for battle; whilst this disposal was

---

[1] By John Clarke, who styles himself First Lieutenant of Marines.
See Introduction, *note*.

effecting, Lieutenant-general Gage ordered the artillery on the Boston side to bombard and set fire to Charlestown, in order to cut off the resource or refuge it might afford the provincials. These orders were executed with incredible dispatch; and the whole town, containing about three hundred houses and a large church, represented a general conflagration by half after two.

By this time the troops were all drawn up in order of battle, when Major-general Howe addressed the officers and soldiers in the following manner:—

GENTLEMEN,—I am very happy in having the honor of commanding so fine a body of men. I do not in the least doubt but that you will behave like Englishmen, and as becometh good soldiers.

If the enemy will not come from their intrenchments, we must drive them out at all events, otherwise the town of Boston will be set on fire by them.

I shall not desire one of you to go a step farther than where I go myself at your head.

Remember, gentlemen, we have no recourse to any resources if we lose Boston but to go on board our ships, which will be very disagreeable to us all.

We then began to proceed to action, by marching with a quick step up the precipice that led to the intrenched provincial army, until within five hundred yards of them; a very brisk fire commenced on their side, and was returned on ours; still marching up to their intrenchments as fast as possible, from whence we dislodged them by four o'clock, the battle being fought and gained within one hour.

In the intrenchments were found five pieces of cannon and five iron swivel guns, which they had taken out of the "Diana" schooner, which they burnt.

The fate of the battle was very severe on the 52d regiment of foot and the first brigade of marines, the officers and men behaving remarkably well, and gaining immortal honor, though with considerable loss, as will appear by the number of the officers killed and wounded.

A full half-hour after the Americans were dislodged from their intrenchments, and it was generally supposed that no enemy were at hand, Lieutenant Dutton, of the 38th regiment, being much afflicted with the gout and severely fatigued with the engagement, sat down on the grass to change his stockings, and while so doing, was alarmed by his servant telling him two men were approaching with firelocks, who were not of the king's troops. The servant expressed an apprehension of their intention being hostile, which Mr. Dutton laughed at, and replied, he supposed they were coming to surrender and give up their arms; but his incredulity proved fatal to him, for they were no sooner within a convenient space than they lodged the contents of their muskets in the bodies of the hard-fated lieutenant and servant, notwithstanding that the king's troops were within fifty yards of him when he lost his life, and some of the light-infantry quite close to him; however, they were instantaneously sacrificed to his much-injured *manes*. Mrs. Dutton and her two children came home in the "Cerberus."

The Americans being defeated, and the king's troops in possession of the intrenchments, Major-general Howe sent to Lieutenant-general Gage for a reinforcement of troops, who immediately sent him four regiments of foot and the second battalion of marines, a company of artillery, and six pieces of cannon.

As soon as the reinforcements of troops arrived, they immediately began to fortify Bunker's Hill; by which they acquired about one hundred and forty acres of fine land, with all the gardens and orchards belonging to Charlestown. This acquisition is of the utmost consequence to Boston, as that town can now be supplied with plenty of vegetables and fruit.

It is impossible to give an exact account of the number which was killed of the Americans: above two hundred were killed on forcing the intrenchments, as appeared on our burying so many; above forty were made prisoners, and carried to Boston jail, where they still remain.

The next day, also, we found a piece of ground, about twenty yards long and twelve wide, which appeared to have been freshly digged. On opening part of it, about two feet deep, a number of dead bodies were discovered, buried in their cloaths; these men must have been killed by the shot and bombs from the shipping the day before, and during part of the night; but, not opening all the piece of ground, the exact number could not be discovered.

A LIST OF OFFICERS KILLED AND WOUNDED ON SATUR-
DAY, THE 17TH OF JUNE, 1775.

4th Regiment.	Captain Balfour	Wounded.
,,	,, West	W.
,,	Lieutenant Barron	W.
,,	,, Brown	W.
5th Regiment.	Major Mitchel	W.
,,	Captain Downs	Killed.
,,	,, Jackson	W.
,,	,, Marsden	W.
,,	Lieutenant Croker	W.
,,	,, M'Clintock	W.
,,	Ensign Charlton	W.
,,	,, Palaguire	W.
10th Regiment.	Captain Fitzgerald	W.
,,	,, Parsons	W.
,,	Lieutenant Pettigrew	W.
,,	,, Hamilton	W.
,,	,, Kelly	W.
,,	,, Verner	W.
14th Regiment.	Lieutenant Bruere, a volunteer	K.
,,	Ensign Haskett	W.
18th Regiment.	Lieutenant Richardson	W.
22d Regiment.	Lieutenant-colonel Abercrombie	W.
23d Regiment.	Captain Blakeney	W.
,,	Lieutenant Cockran	W.
,,	,, Beckwith	W.

23d Regiment.	Lieutenant Lenthall	W.
35th Regiment.	Captain Lyon	W.
,,	,, Drew	W.
,,	Lieutenant Bard	K.
,,	,, Massey	W.
,,	,, Campbel	W.
38th Regiment.	Major Bruce	W.
,,	Captain Boyd	W.
,,	,, Coker	W.
,,	Lieutenant Dutton	K.
,,	,, Christie	W.
,,	,, House	W.
,,	,, Myers	W.
,,	Quarter-master Mitchell	W.
,,	Ensign Serjeant	W.
43d Regiment.	Major Spendlove	W.
,,	Captain Mackenzie	K.
,,	Lieutenant Robertson	W.
,,	,, Dalrymple	W.
47th Regiment.	Major Smelt	W.
,,	Captain England	W.
,,	,, Craigg	W.
,,	,, Allcock	W.
,,	Lieutenant Gold	K.
,,	,, Hilliard	K.
,,	,, Hilier	K.
,,	,, England	W.
52d Regiment.	Major Williams	K.
,,	Captain Addison	K.
,,	,, Davidson	K.
,,	,, Smith	K.
,,	,, Nelson	W.
,,	Lieutenant Higgins	K.
,,	,, Crawford	W.
,,	,, Thompsson	W.
,,	Ensign Chetwynd	W.
,,	,, Grame	W.

59th Regiment.	Lieutenant Haynes	W.
63d Regiment.	Captain Horsford	W.
63d Regiment.	Captain Foillett	W.
„	Lieutenant Dalrymple	K.
65th Regiment.	Major Butler	W.
„	Captain Hudson	K.
„	„ Sinclair	W.
„	Lieutenant Pexton	W.
„	„ Smith	W.
„	„ Hales	W.
67th Regiment.	Captain Sherwin, aide-de-camp	
	to Major-general Howe	K.

MARINES.

Marines.	Major Pitcairn	K.
„	Captain Campbel	K.
„	„ Ellis	K.
„	„ Chudleigh	W.
„	„ Logan	W.
„	„ Averne	W.
„	Capt.-lieutenant and Adj. Johnson	W.
„	First Lieutenant Finnie	K.
„	„ „ Shea	K.
„	„ „ Gardner	K.
„	„ „ Brisbane	W.
„	„ „ Ragg	W.
„	„ „ Pitcairn	W.
„	Second Lieutenant Dyer	W.
„	Engineer Page	W.
Artillery.	Captain Limoine	W.
„	„ Huddleston	W.
„	Lieutenant Shutworth	W.
„	„ Campbell	W.

Field officers killed	3
„ „ wounded	4
Captains killed	9
„ wounded	25
Subalterns killed	11
„ wounded	40
Total of officers	92

Non-commissioned officers and private men	Killed	200
	Wounded	749
Total of officers and men		1041

REGIMENTS IN THE FIELD OF BATTLE ON THE 17TH OF JUNE, 1775.

Fifth,	Fifty-second,
Thirty-eighth,	First battalion of marines,
Forty-third,	Thirteen companies of grenadiers,
Forty-seventh,	Thirteen companies of light-infantry.

Besides these regiments which are now in Boston, there are only two more in all America,— the 7th, or Royal English Fusileers, and the 8th.

As it is very uncommon that such a great number of officers should be killed and wounded more than in proportion to the number of private men: the following discovery seems to account for it.

Before the intrenchments were forced, a man, whom the Americans called a marksman, or rifleman, was seen standing upon something near three feet higher than the rest of the troops, as their hats were not visible. This man had no sooner discharged one musket, than another was handed to him, and continued firing in that manner for ten or twelve minutes. And in that small space of time, by their handing to him fresh loaded muskets, it is supposed that he could not kill or wound less than twenty officers; for it was at them particularly that he directed his aim, as was afterwards confirmed by the prisoners. But he soon paid his tribute, for, upon being noticed, he was killed by the grenadiers of the Royal Welsh Fusileers.

Another remarkable circumstance of the heat of this action is, that all the grenadiers of the 4th, or King's Own, regiment were killed or wounded, except four; and of the grenadiers, also of the 23d, or Royal Welsh Fusileers, only three remained, who were not either killed or wounded. The number of men in each company, if complete, should be thirty-nine. This disproportion also is very great, as, from calculations of most pitched battles, the proportion of the number of killed and wounded is only every eighth man.

As soon as the news of the battle being over reached Boston, those persons who style themselves friends to government instantly sent out every sort of carriage they had, as coaches, chariots, single-horse chaises, and even hand-barrows, to the water-side, to assist in bringing to Boston the wounded and killed officers and soldiers to their respective homes; likewise all the physicians, surgeons, and apothecaries of Boston instantly attended the wounded officers, and gave them every assistance in their power.

Then followed a melancholy scene of several carriages, with the dead and dying officers; in the first of which was Major Williams bleeding and dying, and three dead captains of the 52d regiment; but he lived till the next morning.

The second contained four dead officers, then another with wounded officers; and this scene continued until Sunday morning, before all the wounded private men could be brought to Boston.

Those soldiers who fell in the field were instantly buried there; and on Monday morning all the dead officers were decently buried in Boston, in a private manner, in the different churches and church-yards there. Lieutenant-colonel Abercrombie and Major Pitcairn were buried in the King's Chapel.

During the engagement, a captain of marines, who had been in several, remarked to Major Pitcairn that of all the actions he had been in, this was the hottest: first, from the burning of the houses in Charlestown; next, the heat of the day; and, thirdly, from the heat of the enemy's fire. The Major answered him that soldiers should inure themselves to all manner of hardships, not to regard either heat or cold; "for my part, at present (says he), I have enough to do to mind my duty, which I shall do to the utmost of my power." Soon after, they were both of them shot through the body, and died instantly.

A report having prevailed that Doctor Warren was not killed, I think it necessary to contradict it, as I saw a soldier, after the Doctor was wounded and lying in the trenches, going to run him through the body with his bayonet; on which the Doctor desired he would not kill him, for he was much wounded, and could not live a great while louger; on which the soldier swore that he would, for that he had done more mischief than any one else; and immediately run him through the body.

The Doctor's dress was a light-colored coat, with a white satin waistcoat laced with silver, and white breeches, with silver loops, which I saw the soldier soon after strip off his body.

He was supposed to be the commander of the American army that day; for General Putnam was about three miles distance, and formed an ambuscade with about three thousand men.

As it was imagined that the Americans would give great encouragement to the king's troops to induce them to desert, by offering them lands to cultivate, it had its effect upon some, as upwards of one hundred of the 18th regiment, or Royal Irish, deserted, and are still with them; two or three of these indeed returned to the regiment, as the Americans had not performed their agreement.

A soldier, also, of the 4th regiment came to his captain and told him that an offer was made him of ten dollars and a new suit of clothes, on condition of his deserting; that, if he approved of it, he would take the money, go as a spy, and at a short but convenient opportunity would return again to the regiment, and inform him how he was treated. The captain approved of the soldier's plan, and consented. The soldier staid about a week with them, but had his money and clothes taken from him, and put to hard labor, instead of other encouragement.

The quartermaster-sergeant of the 38th regiment went off with about forty pounds of his captain's money, and has been appointed a lieutenant-colonel in their service, and is one of the most active men which they have.

A corporal from the marines, on board the "Lively" man-of-war, also deserted, and has been appointed captain and adjutant.

Desertion, however, has now taken its leave; for since the Americans came to a resolution, on the 19th of April last, to abridge the king's troops from fresh provisions from the country, the soldiers are so exasperated against them, that not one attempts to desert; nor does soldier or sailor think of it now.

A remarkable instance of benevolence and humanity was shown by General Gage's lady, the day after the action, which ought never to be forgotten. She sent all her fowls, fish, and what little fresh meat she had in the house, to the wounded officers, scarcely leaving a sufficiency for herself and the General. This is not all: her goodness and charity to the soldiers' wives and children have gained her immortal honor, which she very justly merits. As a general benevolence for the army is very characteristic of the English ladies, I hope they will follow General Gage's lady's most amiable example. Within this month are expected home some hundreds of poor unfortunate soldiers and their families from Boston, some with one leg, others with one arm, some without either leg or arm. When you see any of these men, consider what they have suffered; if it were possible, it would draw tears from iron and steel.

On my arrival in London, I heard almost everybody declare their surprise that Earl Percy's name should not be mentioned by Lieutenant-general Gage. With what propriety could he introduce the name of any officer, however distinguished his rank might be, if he was not in the action? I shall therefore explain the reason why, although his regiment was in the action, he could not with propriety charge at the head of it.

On the arrival at Boston of the three generals lately sent

out in the "Cerberus" man-of-war,—Major-general Howe, Major-general Clinton, Major-general Burgoyne,—the army, according to the military establishment, was divided into three brigades, under ea h of their respective commanders. Every brigade has a brigadier-general, but whose rank only exists while upon service.

Under Major-general Howe was Colonel Pigot.
        "   "   Clinton, Colonel Earl Percy.
        "   "   Burgoyne, Colonel Jones.

Brigadier-general Earl Percy deserves the greatest encomiums that is possible for pen to write in his praise. His unbounded generosity and general benevolence exceed all I ever saw. When one considers the noble race of ancestors from whence he is descended, I cannot be at a loss to account for his noble and princely spirit, which causes him to be esteemed by his officers and adored by his men, as he makes it his perpetual study to do all the good possible to everybody.

————

A LIST OF THE MEN-OF-WAR NOW AT BOSTON, WHERE STATIONED, AND THE NUMBER OF GUNS ON BOARD EACH SHIP.

The "Preston," of 50 guns, Admiral Graves, Captain Robinson, near Boston.

The "Somerset," of 70 guns, Captain Le Cras, between Boston and Charlestown.

The "Lively," of 20 guns, Captain Bishop, between the islands, at the entrance of the harbor.

The "Glasgow," of 20 guns, Captain Howe, at the upper end of the river, between Boston and Charlestown.

The "Falcon," sloop, of 16 guns, Captain Linzee, at the mouth of Cape Cod Bay.

The "Boyne," of 70 guns, Captain Hartwell, near the castle, about two leagues from Boston.

With several schooners and armed ships, to examine all ships going in and out.

These ships, from the natural situation of Boston, are a very great defence to the town; nor can it be annoyed by the

Americans, without a superior naval force; they, however, had the hardiness, on Sunday, the 28th of May, whilst the chaplain on board the "Somerset" was at prayers, to come down to the shore from William's Island, and fired several musket shots, which hit the ship, but did no mischief. The compliment was returned by a discharge of grape-shot, but, they believe, without any effect, as none were seen to drop; and they immediately made a precipitate retreat, but in sight of us set William's house on fire.

A most horrid plot, also, was discovered of their intending to massacre all the officers in Boston in one night. The officers being quartered in private lodgings, an alarm was to be given in the night, and as each officer was coming out of the street-door, he was to be assassinated; but happily the affair was discovered before it was put in execution. A boy, seen swimming across the river between Boston and Charlestown, gave a suspicion he was carrying some intelligence; he was accordingly taken up and examined, when, after some time, a letter was found in his stocking-foot, which led to the discovery.

As everybody is anxious for the fate of the town of Boston, on account of the king's troops being in it, and their opinions being very various in regard to the possibility of its holding out against the American army, an account of its situation, strength, &c., may not be improper, as from this account the public may form a better judgment of it.

Boston is the capital of New England; lies in long. 71°5′ W., lat. 42° 24′ N.; and although London is in lat. 51° 30′N., yet the winters are much severer there than at London, and the harbor is generally frozen up; the summers, also, are hotter.

It is situated on a peninsula, at the bottom of a fine bay, and is joined to the continent by a neck of land, which forms a road near one mile in length, which has lately been fortified in a very strong manner with redoubts, *chevaux de frize,* and a large number of cannon. This is the only avenue to the town on the land side.

The town contains between four and five thousand houses, and about twenty thousand inhabitants; but near two-thirds of these are supposed to have quitted it, and gone to other parts of America, or joined their army; and most of those who are left profess themselves steady friends to government.

The laws relating to the poor are upon such a plan that there are no beggars in any part of America.

The account of the Scotch soldier being killed by his brother at Charlestown, as mentioned in the "Gazetteer" of the 7th of August, I rather think has been manufactured here by some news-collector, as I never heard the least account of it whilst at Boston.

About the harbor the town forms the shape of a crescent, and the country rising gradually behind it, affords a very agreeable prospect. It is surrounded by a number of islands, on one of which, at about a league distance, is built a castle to command the entrance of the harbor, and is very well fortified.

The entrance into the harbor is not wide enough for above three sail at a time, but is capable of containing above five hundred sail.

A pier has been built at the bottom of the bay, near seven hundred yards long, on the north of which is built a row of warehouses for the use of the merchants; and the water is so very deep that they can conveniently unload without the help of boats.

The streets are very commodious and large, particularly that which extends from the town-house to the pier.

Across Charles River, directly opposite Boston, Charlestown is situated on a peninsula, which contained about three hundred houses, a church, and some public buildings.

A ferry is established across the river, which is about two hundred yards wide, for the ready communication between the two towns.

The only possible method of annoying Boston was from this quarter; but since Lieutenant-general Gage has been in possession of it, he has been fortifying it very strongly towards the peninsula; and whilst he keeps possession of it, Boston cannot be set on fire except by those on the inside of it.

The American army have also begun to fortify a hill at a small distance, called Prospect Hill. At present they have not been uniformly clothed, but both officers and soldiers wore their own clothes; nor did I see any colors to their regiments on the day of action. Their firelocks are very long, some near seven feet; and they had fifes and drums. Their men are in general very robust, and larger than the English.

In this situation, by the latest accounts, are the two armies; but if any material occurrences happen, the author, having settled a correspondence at Boston, will give the public a further account of them, and would take it as a very particular obligation to be informed of any by a line, directed for him at Mr. Millan's, bookseller, at Whitehall.

As thirty-six years of the author's life have been spent in the service of his late and present Majesty, he hopes that the indulgent public and the curious critic will therefore look upon him as a soldier, not as a writer, and excuse any incorrectness in his language, or defect of style, as what he has aimed at has only been to give a plain narrative of real facts; if he gives satisfaction in that, he will think himself completely happy.

POSTSCRIPT.

Having promised the public to communicate any intelligence that I might receive from America, I have the pleasure of presenting them with extracts from three letters just received: two from Boston, the other from Savannah, in Georgia; the last of which shows how fast the spirit of opposition to government is travelling through the whole continent of America, as now the two Floridas only are wanting to complete the whole continent, from Boston to the south being engaged.

BOSTON, July 18, 1775.

Every thing here at present is quiet; and it is thought by almost everybody that each side will remain on the defensive during the remainder of the summer, in order to see what pacific negotiations may produce during the winter, and particularly to wait the decision of the British Parliament.

The Americans still continue to throw up fortifications at a small distance from Bunker's Hill, to prevent the regulars from advancing on that side.

It has been reported that Lieutenant-general Gage and Admiral Graves are ordered home; but you may depend upon it, that there is not the least foundation for such a report; however, Major-general Burgoyne is certainly going to England very soon.

The following anecdote of British valor in a grenadier of the 63d regiment I am confident will give you pleasure:—

Captain Horsford having been wounded, and Lieutenant Dalrymple killed, a serjeant of the grenadiers told the private men, ou now see, my lads, that our brave captain is greatly wounded, and the lieutenant killed; now, I have the honor to command you; therefore let us get into their trenches as fast as possibly we can, for we must either conquer or die. The serjeant upon this, and the few men whom he had left, were the first who entered the redoubt of the provincial army. Lieutenant-general Gage, for this brave behavior, has recommended him to his Majesty; and it is thought that his Majesty will honor the serjeant with a commission in one of the regiments here.

BOSTON, July 23, 1775.

A detachment from the provincial army has very lately made a descent on Long Island, carried off all the cattle, and burnt about sixty houses. They also destroyed the light-house at the entrance of the harbor, which will prove of great detriment to the shipping.

As fresh provisions and vegetables have lately been so very scarce, it has had a bad effect on the health of the inhabitants; and they already feel it, by beginning to be afflicted with the scurvy. This has induced many of the best families to think of quitting, and they are preparing to sail for England.

Although the American army does not seem to be disposed for acting offensively this campaign, yet they are taking every step necessary for making a vigorous defence against the next.

SAVANNAH, GEORGIA, June 10, 1775.

This place is so involved in the American disputes that I am afraid it will be ruined. A number of mad-headed fellows (who call themselves Sons of Liberty), headed by a merchant or two of this place, two nights before the king's birthday, tumbled the cannons from the battery down the bank of the river, that they might not fire on that day, and spiked up the touch-holes of every one of them; and because some captains of vessels, with their men, and other well-affected gentlemen of the town, with indefatigable pains, and after working the whole night, got them up again, they had the assurance to go to some and write to others to leave the province in seven days. Next Tuesday the time expires, and they seem determined to compel them to go; but we are resolved to oppose them with all our power.

They even went to a house on Monday, when the governor and council were dining together, and, a large body of them having assembled, set up what they call a Liberty-Tree, with a white flag, under which they discharged forty-five guns, and drank success to the American arms. You may be sure I was not to be idle at seeing such proceedings, and, being a little elevated with drinking his Majesty's health, got into the scuffle, lost my hat and wig, and in return brought away a black eye, a swelled lip, and lost a little of the bark of my nose.

The country people are flocking in to their assistance; but those who intend to support the governor in opposing their unlawful attempts are to meet him and the council to-morrow, to concert methods for opposing them; and I assure you I intend to make one at the meeting; and our number will be nearly equal, it is imagined.

OFFICERS DEAD OF THEIR WOUNDS.

Captain Averne, of the marines.
Captain Lyon, of the 35th regiment.
Lieutenant Thompson, of the 52d regiment.
Major Spendlove, of the 43d regiment.
Lieutenant Verner, of the 10th regiment.

8

PROMOTIONS IN AMERICA SINCE JUNE 17, 1775.

Regiment.

4th.	Halcott, Lieutenant	vice Rooke	Preferred.
,,	Fish, Quartermaster	,, Rooke	
,,	Butler, Lieutenant	,, Knight	Killed.
,,	Kemble, Ensign	,, Butler	
5th.	Smith, Captain	,, Downes	Deceased.
,,	Baker, Captain-lieutenant	,, Smith	
,,	Minchin, Lieutenant	,, Baker	
,,	England, Ensign	,, Minchin	
,,	Charlton, Lieutenant	,, Jackson	Deceased.
14th.	Browne, Lieutenant	,, Bruere	Killed.
,,	Grant, Ensign	,, Browne	
22d.	Campbell, Lieutenant-col.	,, Abercromby	Deceased.
,,	French, Major	,, Campbell	
,,	Handfield, Captain	,, French	
,,	Fenner, Captain-lieut.	,, Handfield	
,,	Forter, Ensign	,, French	
35th.	Ross, Lieutenant	,, Pringle	Deceased.
	Madden, Ensign	,, Ross	
''	Lamb, Lieutenant	,, Bard	Killed.
''	Shaw, Ensign	,, Lamb	
38th.	Sargent, Lieutenant	,, Dutton	Killed.
,,	Dorcus, Ensign	,, Sargent	
,,	Moncrieffe, Ensign	,, Halcot	Preferred.
43d.	Dawson, Lieutenant	,, Hull	Deceased.
,,	Rivers, Ensign	,, Dawson	
	Poe, Lieutenant	,, Gold	Deceased.
,,	Bunbury, Ensign	,, Poe	
,,	Baldwin, Lieutenant	,, Hilliard	Killed.
,,	Dowling, Ensign	,, Baldwin	
52d.	Humphreys, Major	,, Williams	Killed.
,,	Neilson, Captain	,, Humphreys	
,,	Crawford, Captain	,, Addison	Killed.
,,	Thompson, Captain	,, Davison	,,
,,	Rooke, Captain	,, Smith	,,
,,	Mackilwaine, Capt-lieut.	,, Neilson	

Regiment.

52d.	Hunter, Lieutenant	vice Mackilwaine.
,,	Chetwynd, Lieutenant	,, Crawfurd.
,,	Fuge, Lieutenant	,, Thompson.
,,	Graeme, Lieutenant	,, Higgins . Deceased.
,,	Harrison, Ensign	,, Hunter.
,,	Vans, Ensign	,, Chetwynd.
,,	Brookes, Ensign	,, Fuge.
,,	Mackay, Adjutant	,, Graeme.
59th.	Gordon, Quartermaster	,, Owen . . Deceased.
63d.	Roberts, Lieutenant	,, Dalrymple Killed.
,,	Drury, Ensign	,, Roberts.
65th.	Watson, Captain	,, Hudson . Killed.
,,	Baylie, Lieutenant	,, Watson.
,,	Hardy, Ensign	,, Baylie.

MARINES.

Major Chudleigh	vice Pitcairn.
,, Souter	,, Short.
Captain Lindsay	,, Chudleigh.
,, A. Walker	,, Souter.
,, Ross	,, Campbell.
,, D. Johnston	,, Ellis.
Capt.-lieut. J. Adair	,, Lindsay.
,, Sir J. Dalston	,, Walker.
,, Hadden	,, Ross.
,, Pitcairn	,, Johnston.

First Lieutenants.

Lewis	Potter
Robert Moore	Cary
Thos. Woodcock	Ronald McDonald

Tantum.

Second Lieutenants.

Bowman	Dunbar
Morrison	Forester
Moriarty	Dexter

Fortescue.

CHAPTER X

BATTLE OF BUNKER HILL

X.

BATTLE OF BUNKER HILL.[1]

BY A BRITISH SOLDIER.

T HE seventeenth, at break of day,
  The Yankees did surprise us
With the strong works they had thrown up,
To burn the town and drive us.

But soon we had an order come,
  An order to defeat them;
With three good flints and sixty rounds,
  Each soldier hoped to beat them.

At noon we marched to the Long Wharf,
  Where boats were ready waiting;
With expedition we embarked,
  Our ships kept cannonading.

And soon our boats all filled were,
  With officers and soldiers,
With as good troops as England had,
  T' oppose who dared control us.

And when our boats all filled were,
  We rowed in line of battle;
With grenadiers and infantry,
  While grape-shot loud did rattle.

---

[1] This was written by a common soldier, who deserted to the Americans, and used to sing it in their camps. Benjamin Russell, who repeated it to a friend, declared it perfectly accurate in its facts.

And when we landed on the shore,
  We formed in line together;
The Yankee boys then manned their works,
  And swore we shouldn't come thither.

Brave General Howe, on our right wing,
  Cried, "Boys, fight on like thunder;
You soon shall see these rebels flee,
  With great amaze and wonder."

But such stout Whigs I never saw;
  To hang them all I'd rather,
Than mow their hay with musket balls
  And buck-shot mixed together.

As for their king, that John Hancock,
  And Adams, if they're taken,
Their heads for signs we'll raise aloft
  Upon their hill called Beacon.

But our conductor, he got broke,
  For his misconduct, sure, sir;
The shot he sent for twelve-pound guns
  Were made for twenty-fours, sir.

CHAPTER XI

BATTLE OF BUNKER HILL

XI.

THE BATTLE OF BUNKER HILL.[1]

MEANWHILE, the British forces held at bay,
　　Coop'd up in Boston, there inactive lay;
But reinforc'd and scorning dull repose,
They rouz'd t' attack their bold surrounding foes.
Determin'd now their enemies t' offend,
Beyond their former bounds their lines t' extend;
The chiefs resolv'd to seize on Bunker's hill,
Which amply prov'd their military skill.
Ere the detatchment to the place was sent,
Their foes advanc'd to frustrate their intent;
For under covert of the friendly night,
Warren had seiz'd, and fortify'd that height;
The colonists must be dislodg'd from thence,
Whatever was the dreadful consequence;
About two thousand were embark'd to go
'Gainst the redoubt, and formidable foe;
The Lively's, Falcon's, Fame's, and Glasgow's roar,
Cover'd their landing on the destin'd shore;
They form'd, and part towards the trenches sped;
Th' intrepid Howe those vet'ran forces led.
The trenches, and redoubt, were trebly mann'd,
Howe wisely made a necessary stand;
For reinforcements sent, soon as he view'd
The well-arm'd, congregating multitude,

---

[1] This fragment is extracted from a poem entitled "The American War," by George Cockings, printed in London, in 1781. It is not found in any American authority I have seen.

We may conclude he thus the troops address'd
(Whose flagging spirits seemed to be depress'd),
March boldly on, your cause is just, and good,
Th'insurgents have the parliament withstood,
The legislature's acts have set aside,
And have Great Britain's martial power defy'd!
The British chiefs began to pant for fame,
Their souls were full of emulating flame;
Prepar'd t' advance to stem the growing tide
Of thousands, rushing in on ev'ry side.
Well pleas'd the gen'ral look'd around and saw
The sympathetic manly martial glow
He ceas'd, and fac'd towards the strong redoubt,
The troops sent forth a loud approving shout;
Not that exulting shout, when they advance
'Gainst Spanish foes, or vet'ran troops of France;
But on they march'd, to give the dreadful storm;
And do whatever mortals could perform!
On Boston's shore, Burgoyne and Clinton stood
And ev'ry movement of the forces view'd,
Prepar'd to speed their timely aid to lend,
Or from the spot destructive war to send;
They learn'd that Charles-town must be wrapp'd in flame
Or Britain's troops retire with tarnish'd fame,
Another corps 'gainst Charles-town made a stand,
With good provincial troops completely mann'd;
Here the firm animating Pigot fought,
His warlike flame the gallant leaders caught;
The privates felt its force, from man to man,
T' excel in fight an emulation ran.
They steadily advanc'd, on conquest bent;
A mortal show'r of lead incessant sent;
Th' Americans likewise for conquest burn'd,
And a like mortal show'r of lead return'd;
Maintain'd the town, and resolutely strove
To harass Howe, as up the hill he drove;
But vex'd by bursting shells, and show'rs of balls,
Or crushed by falling roofs or batter'd walls,

They felt discomfiture; and now there came
A flight of shells, fraught with destructive flame!
A scene ensu'd might fill the brave with dread;
From house to house the conflagration spread;
Ear-piercing shrieks; heart-rending groans, and cries;
And terrifying shouts of vict'ry rise;
Amidst the desolating wild uproar,
Forth rush'd th' inhabitants from ev'ry door;
To sex, nor age, no place an azyle yields;
In crouds they ran and sought th' adjacent fields;
Swifter than they the rapid bullets flew,
And some ill-fated persons overthrew;
From hope excluded, in a wild dismay,
The town untenable, the troops gave way;
To Bunker's Hill they fled, and in their rear,
In close pursuit, the regulars drew near;
The trenches gain'd, they fac'd and made a stand,
And intermix'd with Warren's chosen band;
Follow'd by Pigot with a martial frown,
Wrapp'd in the vapour of the burning town.

For battle warm'd with military skill,
Howe led two thousand up the dang'rous hill,
Where hostile parties under covert lay,
T' impede his march, and strike with cold dismay,
Now, Warren frowning rouz'd (erect he stood),
From right to left, his must'ring forces view'd;
From man to man, he saw with great delight,
Resentment flash'd, with readiness to fight;
Prepar'd to speak, the troops attentive hung
On the persuasive accents of his tongue.
Now, my brave friends, your innate worth display;
Great Britain's regulars advance this way;
Soldiers, and sailors, seem dispos'd around,
To drive us from this advantageous ground;
Th' artill'ry's landed on th' adjacent shore,
Their naval thunder hath begun to roar;

On Bostons shore their batteries they ply;
From whence the show'rs of shells incessant fly;
Already Charles-town at their mercy lies;
The lambent flames and clouds of smoke arise;
That obstacle no longer proves a bar;
And this way comes the tumult of the war.
Tho' Gage ten thousand well-train'd troops may boast,
Join'd by the British fleet t' infest our coast;
Tho' 'mongst their chiefs (vet'rans in war renown'd),
Howe, Clinton, Pigot and Burgoyne, are found;
Tho' Pitcairne's, Montcrief's, Abercrombie's name,
Tho' gallant Percy's, swells the list of fame;
Tho' Sherwin, Addison, Page, Bruce and Small,
Attend on Howe, at honour's glorious call;
Tho' Williams, Campbell, Smith, with many more,
Skilful in war now tread th' Atlantic shore;
Tho' steady Carleton widely spreads alarms,
And Dunmore our Virginian negroes arms;
I see no cause for fear my friends, since we
Have Putnam, Pribble, Washington and Lee;
Arnold, Montgom'ry, Gates, Macpherson bold,
Already in the list of fame inroll'd;
Lamb, Wooster, Schuyler, Hendricks, Cheeseman, go
With these, in Canada, to fight the foe;
We've Woodford 'gainst Dunmore; we've Gardner too,
Who stands determin'd now within your view;
Ward, Prescott, Thomas, Heath, and more beside,
Will stand the test whene'er in battle tried.
I grant it may prove difficult to bar,
The dreadful progress of Great Britain's war!
Whatever single state provokes her frown,
Shrinks from her war; and trembles for the crown;
United France and Spain have often felt
The vengeance which her troops and tars have dealt;
But then, we sent her from our friendly shores,
Provisions, timber, ships, and naval stores;
And in her quarrel (on the continent),
We risk'd our lives; our blood, and treasure spent;

Now, we are torn from her dismember'd side;
Twelve rising states in arms, her claims deny'd;
And her (European) neighb'ring states around,
In private wish we were with conquest crown'd;
Will fraudful smile on her, will us befriend;
And under covert their assistance lend.
Like to th' invaders of our native land,
We station'd here on the defence to stand;
From Wales, Great Britain and Hibernia sprung;
Our nerves for war, with equal vigor strung;
Our hearts as firm as theirs, our blood the same,
Which swells our veins, and animates each frame;
Th' event with perseverance let us wait,
Some wish'd for change, a terrible defeat;
Or providential stroke of mighty fate,
May all our daring foes intimidate;
To Heav'n appealing, we for succour fly,
And for success on Providence rely;
I doubt not but we shall experience yet,
"Qui nos transtulit, semper sustinet."
Altho' shou'd be by ruling Heav'n decreed,
We shall at present unsuccessful bleed;
I forward look compos'd, and firmly trust,
When we are mingled with our kindred dust,
'Tis his decree who rules above the skies
We shall in time a mighty empire rise.
Should Providence ordain that we must fall,
Let us with chearfulness obey the call;
In death, we shall some consolation have,
We sink with honour to the silent grave;
They shouted loud, and made this short reply,
We will be free, or will with honour die.
Meanwhile, the British chiefs the troops inspir'd,
Examples rouz'd, and exhortations fir'd:
And tho' short time in words they chose to waste,
As up the hill they press'd with martial haste,
Whilst they surmounted every hostile bar,
Their deeds aloud proclaim'd them form'd for war.

The charging regulars still nearer drew
'Gainst front, and flank, and hot the battle grew;
Whilst Britain's ships of war maintain'd the fight,
Directing all their fire 'gainst Bunker's height.
On churches, spires and lofty domes around,
On hills adjacent, and each rising ground,
Thronging spectators, anxious thousands stood,
And lost in grand suspense the battle view'd;
A scene of carnage! obstinate the fight!
Tremendous, pleasing, horrid, glorious sight!

Gigantic terrors at the breastwork frown'd;
Solemn and slow, advancing o'er the ground;
The regulars drew near in awful form,
Like Jove attended by a thunder-storm;
They mov'd majestic in a sulph'rous cloud;
Britain's brazen engines bellowing loud;
At the redoubt appear'd no sign of fear,
They brought their brazen thunder well to bear;
On rough defence seem'd resolutely bent;
And down the hill a storm of iron sent:
Long they continu'd thus, and either side,
Howitzers, musquetry, and cannon ply'd,
Whilst 'gainst great obstacles the Britons found,
They strove t' advance, and gain superior ground;
Doubtless, each soldier thought he shou'd contend
With an acquaintance, brother, or a friend!
At least 'gainst countrymen shou'd lift his hand,
Sprung from Great Britain's or Hibernia's land!
Their resolution stagger'd when they saw
The danger still more formidable grow!
And found they must themselves long time expose
To the brisk fire of their well-sheltered foes!
From rifled tubes, to strike the chief's intent,
With deadly aim they leaden mischief sent;
Whilst in conjunction, their artill'ry made
'Gainst Britain's troops, a mortal cannonade;

Who, quite expos'd without the batt'ring aid,
And cover of their cannon were dismay'd;
Thus circumstanc'd the troops had like t' have fled
From the dread spot, where Abererombie led;
Nor did they seem to make a firmer stand,
Where Howe, th' intrepid Howe, bore chief command!
From flank to flank, his anxious looks he cast,
From corps to corps with fearless haste he past;
Travers'd the line of hottest hostile fire;
And by example, strove to reinspire
With resolution, those who seem'd dismay'd,
Irresolute and ready to recede.
Small, Sherwin, Page and Addison, were found,
Where duty call'd, and threat'ning danger frown'd;
Both exhortations and examples fail'd,
A cooling tremor Britain's troops assail'd!
They halted in suspense, at length gave way!
Regardless of the honour of the day!
When the provincial officers beheld
The royal forces stagger'd and repell'd;
Elate with hope, almost with vict'ry crown'd;
They thus address'd their troops which stood around.
They slack their fire! and seem'd to stand at gaze!
Like those whom thunder strikes with vast amaze!
Mark how they thin! on ev'ry side they bleed!
Exert yourselves awhile and on them pour
Of lead and iron mix'd a pond'rous show'r;
No time for recollection let them have,
Convince them North Americans are brave.

    Meanwhile the British persevering chief,
Whose dauntless soul was full of poignant grief;
Alone, and in the rear, retrod the ground;
Oft fac'd about, and grim defiance frown'd,
(So lagg'd firm Ajax in the Grecian rear,
And strove to banish base desponding fear.)
Howe rais'd his voice in an upbraiding tone,
Will Britons flee! and leave their chief alone!

Can you outlive disgrace? the brave disdain
To purchase life by an ignoble stain!
Shall wond'ring nations now exulting hear
The Trans-atlantics fill'd our souls with fear!
Rally, return, and brisk your foes assail;
Your Britain's regulars, and must prevail.
Reluctant, Abercrombie join'd the rout,
Halt, halt, oft call'd aloud, and fac'd about;
Halt, halt, from chief to chief flew round;
Halt, said each officer, and stood his ground;
Oh! shame! they cry'd, that ever shou'd be said,
Great Britain's vet'rans from militia fled!
And left their officers to make th' attack!
Whilst they ran off! or from the fight hung back,
We, to the post of danger first lay claim;
We will stand foremost for each lev'lers aim;
We ask no more than that you'll boldly tread
The path of honour, where you see us lead;
In British annals emulous to shine,
They rang'd in front, a formidable line;
Rush'd on, midst blood, sweat, dust, and smoke, and flame;
And leaders in the truest sense became.
Th' undaunted Pitcairne now their hopes reviv'd;
With him the gallant marine corps arriv'd:
The fifty-second's grenadiers with these,
Rush'd on the palm of victory to seize;
Tho' first humanity their souls possest,
And sentiments fraternal warm'd each breast,
Which made them tardily advance to fight,
And almost to commence inglorious flight;
When they beheld their chiefs and comrades fall,
And heard each leader's animating call;
Saw the marines and Pitcairne passing by,
They fac'd and form'd another charge to try;
Returning ardor banish'd chilling fear;
The chiefs led on; and they brought up the rear;
And now recover'd from their Former dread,
Over the wounded, dying and the dead,

They trod and stumbled with, with indignant speed;
And as they saw their groaning comrades bleed;
A thirst for vengeance and desire for fame,
Fill'd every soul with emulating flame.
When Warren saw them face about, and form,
And onward rush to give another storm;
He stood alarm'd; the consequence he fear'd;
Conceal'd his thoughts, and thus his forces chear'd;
Again recover'd from their cold dismay,
The rally'd British vet'rans move this way;
At the last gasp their fainting courage lies;
The warlike glance forsakes their languid eyes;
Their new rekindling courage soon will fail,
If you stand firm when they the lines assail;
Each face will like Medusa's front appear!
And fill their wav'ring souls again with fear!
From either party as they nearer drew,
Destructive show'rs of balls alternate flew;
In er'ry volley, death triumphant rode;
And thro' the ranks with wasting terror strode;
But for his most delicious morsels sought,
Where Pigot, Howe, Warren, and Gardner fought;
Where Williams, Pitcairne, Abercrombie, turn'd,
He feasted there and there the battle burn'd.

When Pitcairne fell, his son advanc'd in view,
Towards the spot with anxious ardor flew;
Tho' rage and love his steps accelerate,
To guard his father's life he came too late;
Already, death had launch'd his mortal dart
And lodg'd the barb in the bold vet'ran's heart;
Burning for vengeance and oppress'd with grief,
With filial care, he rais'd the wounded chief
From blood and dust (as decency requir'd),
And from the carnage of the field retir'd;
So stain'd with streams of warm paternal gore,
Young Seipio from the field his father bore.

Another son (in this unnat'ral strife)
Was doom'd to see his parent robb'd of life!
Whilst rushing on elate, at glory's call,
With grief imbitter'd by his father's fall,
The gallant Addison suspended stood;
The prostrate dusty sanguin'd ruin view'd;
Too late, like Pitcairne's, came his filial aid;
With looks, where thoughts of vengeance were display'd,
Like him (with sad regret, and tender care)
He bore the lifeless body to the rear;
From mangling feet the cold remains to save,
With warlike pomp committed to the grave.
Howe, Roden, Pigot press'd to closest fight
Warren beheld a dread soul-harrowing sight!
Observ'd his troops preparing to give way;
And mark'd the growing symptoms of dismay!
Aloud he call'd, rouze and shake off your fears;
Partners in fame, my friends, and volunteers;
Bring no disgrace on the provincial arms;
Have children, wives, and liberty no charms!
Your children, wives, and friends, around us wait,
Wound not their souls by shameful base retreat;
Perhaps on us this day, my gallant friends,
The fate of North America depends;
Wou'd you outlive the fight, and see your lands,
And your effects, seiz'd by the victor's hands?
Stung to the quick and full of warlike fire;
We'll die they said, before we will retire;
They shouted loud and for the vict'ry burn'd;
The charging regulars the shout return'd.

Whilst both contending parties (in the strife)
Struggled for victory, for fame, and life;
Clinton with circumspection ready stood,
And a large British reinforcement view'd;
Who seem'd embarrass'd; scarce knew where to speed
With succour in the time of dang'rous need;

Most nobly rouz'd, impatient of delay;
He gain'd the shore, and led the glorious way;
Instant toward the foe, their front they turn'd;
Each caught the flame and for the battle burn'd.
So when Pelides saw the Grecians stand
Irresolutely, on the Phrygian strand,
He join'd his friends with animating glow,
Rouz'd, chear'd, and led them 'gainst th' exulting foe.
Meanwhile, the first assailants, unsustain'd,
'Midst dreadful carnage, had the summit gain'd
Convinc'd they must a rapid effort make,
Their honours, victory and lives at stake.
Examples drew towards the hostile fence,
With more than Ciceronian eloquence;
Come on; come on; the mounting leaders cry'd;
We come; we come; the regulars reply'd:
O'er all impediments they dauntless bound
With Gorgon fronts, and spread dismay around;
Confusion and dispersion soon ensu'd,
Except where Warren and his party stood;
Fierce the provincials fought, and fearless bled,
Where the great oratorial Warren led;
He fac'd grim danger with an heart elate;
At length, a rapid ball came wing'd with fate;
And cut th' intrepid rhetorician down,
Scorning retreat, and panting for renown;
His potent language cou'd the mind controul;
Rekindle fainting courage in the soul;
Cou'd make the coolest troops with ardor glow;
And rush in storms of death upon the foe;
With him the spirit of the battle fled;
From right to left a consternation spread;
On ev'ry side the colonists gave ground;
The regulars indignant gather'd round;
O'er trenches, fences, and each palisade,
A passage like an inundation made;
Bore all resistance down, gain'd the redoubt,
And put the firm provincial troops to rout.

With conquest flush'd, with hard-earn'd vict'ry crown'd,
Brave Howe and Pigot now possess'd the ground,
The rising ground from whence provincials fled;
And up the hill the gallant Clinton led
A reinforcement, which was near at hand,
In hasty march from Charlestown's hostile strand;
Burgoyne observant stood, ready to speed,
Where any shou'd a timely succour need;
And ev'ry soldier long'd at honours call
To grace with dreadful pomp his comrade's fall;
Tho' for success all seemingly combin'd,
With sage precaution Howe the chase declin'd;
With circumspection mov'd, and wou'd not dare,
To hazard a defeat in Putnam's snare.

From the redoubt the lines to Cambridge ran,
Trench lay near trench, and man supported man;
Each eminence was fortifi'd around,
And ambuscades possess'd the lower ground;
Here Putnam, Pribble, Ward, and Thomas stay'd
To check pursuit, and pour in friendly aid;
Prescott and Heath were near with all their force,
T' oppose the victors in their destin'd course.
The diff'rent parties seemed resolv'd t' abide
In each well chosen post they occupy'd;
Altho' their routed friends might help require,
They wou'd not pass the line of naval fire,
Whilst the provincials from their late defeat,
Fil'd off, and strove to make a good retreat;
This to effect they must determin'd push,
As if thro' death's expanded jaws to rush!
A victor foe threaten'd their broken rear;
Frigates and floating batteries lay near,
Across their path, in front, and flank, to rake,
A dreadful, desolating sweep to make;
And cut off ev'ry hope of fresh supply,
Tho' twenty thousand well-arm'd friends were nigh!

10

CHAPTER XII

ORGANIZATION OF THE ROYAL MARINES 1775

XII.

ORGANIZATION OF THE ROYAL MARINES, 1775.

T HE following is an extract from the marine-battalion
orders of the 20th of May, 1775:—
"The Right Honorable the Lords Commissioners of the
Admiralty having directed a reinforcement of marines to serve
under Major Pitcairne in General Gage's army, consisting of
two majors, ten captains, twenty-seven subalterns, two adjutants, one surgeon, two assistant-surgeons, twenty-eight serjeants, twenty-five corporals, twenty drummers, six hundred
privates, the commanding officer deems it necessary, for the
good of the service, to form the whole under his command
into two battalions:—

GRENADIERS.

Officers in First Battalion.   *Officers in Second Battalion.*

Thomas Avarne, captain.   George Logan.
William Finney, 1st lieutenant. Alexander Brisbane.
George Vevers,   Francis Gardner.
,,

First Company.

Stawel Chudleigh, captain.   Hon. John Maitland, captain.
Richard Shea, 1st lieutenant. Jesse Adair, 1st lieut.
——Hewes,   Roland Carter, ,,
,,

Second Company.

Stephen Ellis, captain.   Charles Chandless, captain.
James Robertson, 1st lieut. Fenton Griffiths, 1st lieutenant.
P. D. Robertson, 2d ,,   Henry D'Oyley, 2d ,,

Third Company.

Thomas Lindsay, captain. Thomas Groves, captain.
William Lycett, 1st lieut. John Hadden, 1st lieutenant.
David Collins, 2d „ Titus Conyers, „

Fourth Company.

William Forster, captain. Samuel Davys, captain.
Wm. Graham, 1st lieutenant. Walter Nugent, 1st lieutenant.
Isaac Potter, 2d „ Robert Carey, 2d „

Fifth Company.

Robert Ross, captain. Edward Henvill, captain.
Chas. Steward, 1st lieutenant. Thomas Biggs, 1st lieutenant.
Jonas Matthews, 1st lieut. James Lewis, 2d „

Sixth Company.

William Sabine, captain. George Elliott, captain.
B. M'Donald, 2d lieutenant. Alex. M'Donald, 1st lieut.
Henry Tantum, „ John France, „

Seventh Company.

J. H. Branson, captain. Archer Walker, captain.
Wm. Cresswell, 1st lieut. Jas. Anderson, 1st lieutenant.
Thomas Trollope, 2d „ Robert Moore, 2d „

Eighth Company.

John Percival, captain. John M'Fie, captain.
Aaron Eustace, 1st lieutenant. Sir J. Dalston, Bart., 1st lieut.
Thos. Woodcock, 2d „ Francis Dogherty, „

LIGHT INFANTRY.

W. Souter, captain. Archibald Campbell, captain.
W. Pitcairne, 1st lieutenant. John Dyer, 2d lieutenant.
Philip Howe, 2d „ N. H. Nicholas, 2d lieutenant.

Adjutants.

John Waller, 1st lieutenant. John Fielding, 1st lieutenant.

Quartermasters.

J. Pitcairne, 1st lieutenant. Thomas Smith, 1st lieutenant.

Captain David Johnston, superintendent, adjutant, and
deputy-paymaster to the second battalion.
——Hill, surgeon to the second battalion; William Tervant
and——Silven, surgeon's mates.

The following regulations for the payment of companies
were notified in the battalion orders of the 3d of June:—
"The Right Honorable the Lords Commissioners of the
Admiralty having directed, by their letter to Major Pitcairne,
of the 2d of March last, that the captain of marines commanding companies on shore at Boston should pay their companies in the same manner as practised by the land forces,
the captains or commanding officers of companies will receive
from Captain Johnston, deputy-paymaster, one month's subsistence for the non-commissioned officers and private men of
their respective companies, deducting 1s. 5½d. per week each
for provisions and the usual stoppages, as directed by the Admiralty, viz:—

	$s.$	$d.$
For one serjeant, per week	0	2
„ „ corporal or drummer	0	1½
„ „ private man	0	1
Dollars to be taken at	4	8

Captains are to give the deputy-paymaster complete monthly
pay-rolls, accounting for the subsistence distributed to their
companies, and specifying every particular casualty that has
happened in each company during the preceding month, and
to commence this day."

Cambridge: Press of John Wilson & Son.

Other Colonial History titles offered by *Digital Scanning, Inc.*

New English Canaan,
by Jack Dempsey
As Published in 1999.
TP: 1582181519 ($29.95)
HC: 1582181500 ($39.95)

New English Canaan Text & Notes,
by Thomas Morton
Edited by Jack Dempsey
As Published in 1999.
TP: 158218206X ($15.95)
HC: 1582182078 ($27.95)

Thomas Morton of Merrymount,
by Jack Dempsey
As Published in 1999.
TP: 1582182094 ($21.95)
HC: 1582182108 ($34.95)

Good News From New England,
by Jack Dempsey
As Published in 2001.
TP: 1582187061 ($17.95)
HC: 158218707X ($31.95)

Massasoit of the Wampanoags,
by Alvin G. Weeks
As Published in 1920.
TP: 1582185921 ($14.95)
HC: 158218593X ($27.95)

Watch Fires of '76,
by Samuel A. Drake
As Published in 1895.
TP: 1582184704 ($14.95)
HC: 1582184712 ($29.95)

The History of Philip's War,
by Thomas Church, Esq.
As Published in 1827.
TP: 158218089X ($19.95)
HC: 1582181306 ($29.95)

History of King Philip,
by John Abbott
As Published in 1857.
TP: 1582183147 ($19.95)
HC: 1582183155 ($34.95)

King Philip's War,
by George E. Ellis
and John Morris
As Published in 1906.
TP: 1582184305 ($17.95)
HC: 1582184313 ($29.95)

Round the Hub,
by Samuel A. Drake
As Published in 1882.
TP: 1582185182 ($14.95)
HC: 1582185190 ($27.95)

Border Wars of New England,
by Samuel A. Drake
As Published in 1897.
TP: 1582183325 ($15.95)
HC: 1582183333 ($29.95)

The Making of New England,
by Samuel A. Drake
As Published in 1899.
TP: 1582183988 ($14.95)
HC: 1582183996 ($27.95)

Battle of Bunker Hill,
by George E. Ellis
As Published in 1895.
TP: 158218402X ($9.95)
HC: 1582184038 ($19.95)

The Puritan Age and Rule in Massachusetts 1629-1686,
by George E. Ellis
As Published in 1888.
TP: 1582186200 ($27.95)
HC: 1582186219 ($39.95)

New England Legends and Folk Lore,
by Samuel A. Drake
As Published in 1901.
TP: 1582184429 ($24.95)
HC: 1582184437 ($39.95)

Bunker Hill,
by Samuel A. Drake
As Published in 1875.
TP: 1582183295 ($6.95)
HC: 1582183309 ($19.95)

On Plymouth Rock,
by Samuel A. Drake
As Published in 1897.
TP: 1582184348 ($9.95)
HC: 1582184356 ($24.95)

To order any of the above titles:

* Contact your local bookstore and order through *Ingram Books.*
* Contact the publisher directly
(for general information or special event purchases):
Digital Scanning, Inc.
344 Gannett Rd., Scituate, MA 02066
Phone: (781) 545-2100 Fax: (781) 545-4908 Toll Free in the U.S.: 888-349-4443
email: books@digitalscanning.com
www.digitalscanning.com

Printed in the USA
CPSIA information can be obtained
at www.ICGtesting.com
JSHW080225290723
45459JS00002B/154